LEARNING ABOUT Insects

Catherine Veitch

Raintree

Chicago, Illinois

The author would like to dedicate this book to her mother, Jacqueline Veitch, who inspired her with a love of nature.

© 2014 Raintree
an imprint of Capstone Global Library, LLC
Chicago, Illinois

To contact Capstone Global Library please phone 800-747-4992, or visit our website www.capstone-pub.com

Edited by Dan Nunn, Rebecca Rissman, and Sian Smith
Designed by Joanna Hinton-Malivoire
Picture research by Mica Brancic
Production by Sophia Argyris
Originated by Capstone Global Library Ltd
Printed in the United States of America in Eau Claire, WIsconsin.

112015
009331R

Library of Congress Cataloging-in-Publication Data
Veitch, Catherine.
Learning about insects / Catherine Veitch.—1st ed.
p. cm.—(The natural world)
 Includes bibliographical references and index.
ISBN 978-1-4109-5403-9 (hb)
ISBN 978-1-4109-5408-4 (pb)
1. Insects–Juvenile literature. I. Title. II. Series: Natural world (Chicago, Ill.)

QL467.2.V45 2013
595.7—do23   2012049394

Acknowledgments
Shutterstock: ajt, 16, 22 (top), alslutsky, 10, 23 (bottom), Andrey Pavlov, 4, Anson0618, 8, Biehler Michael, 21 (inset), 23 (top middle), Christian Musat, 7, 22 (bottom), Cosmin Manci, 12, D. Kucharski& K. Kucharska, 19, efendy, 22 (top middle), Eric Isselee, 18 (top), 23 (top), Erkki Alvenmod, 13, erni, 21 (botom), Henrik Larsson, 15, Karel Gallas, 5, 22 (bottom middle), khlungcenter, 11, liou.zojan, 18 (inset), optimarc, 17, Palto, back cover, 14, 23 (bottom middle), PetrP, 9, Rob Hainer, cover, Suede Chen, 20, Vladimir Konjushenko, 6

We would like to thank Michael Bright for his invaluable help in the preparation of this book.

Every effort has been made to contact copyright holders of any material reproduced in this book. Any omissions will be rectified in subsequent printings if notice is given to the publisher.

Contents

Ant

Beetle

Bumblebee

Butterfly

Cockroach

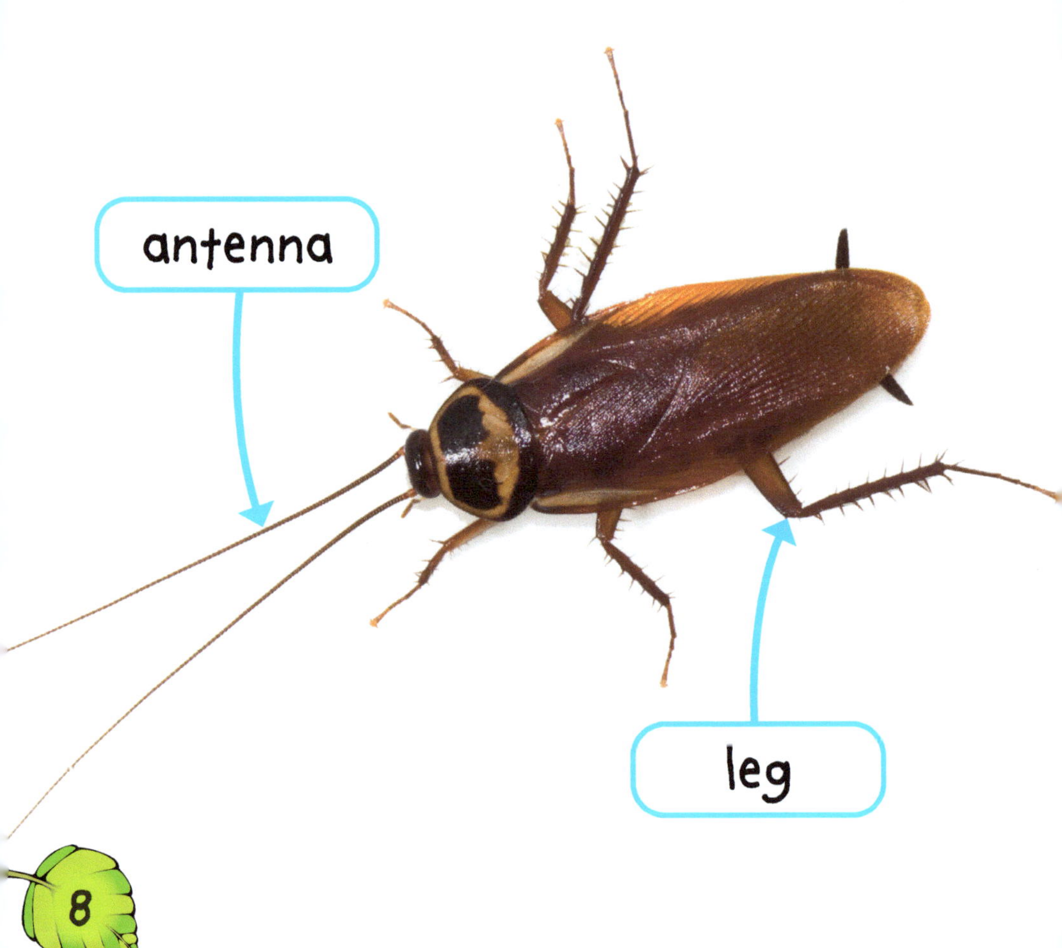

Cricket

Dragonfly

Firefly

Flea

Fly

13

Ladybug

Mosquito

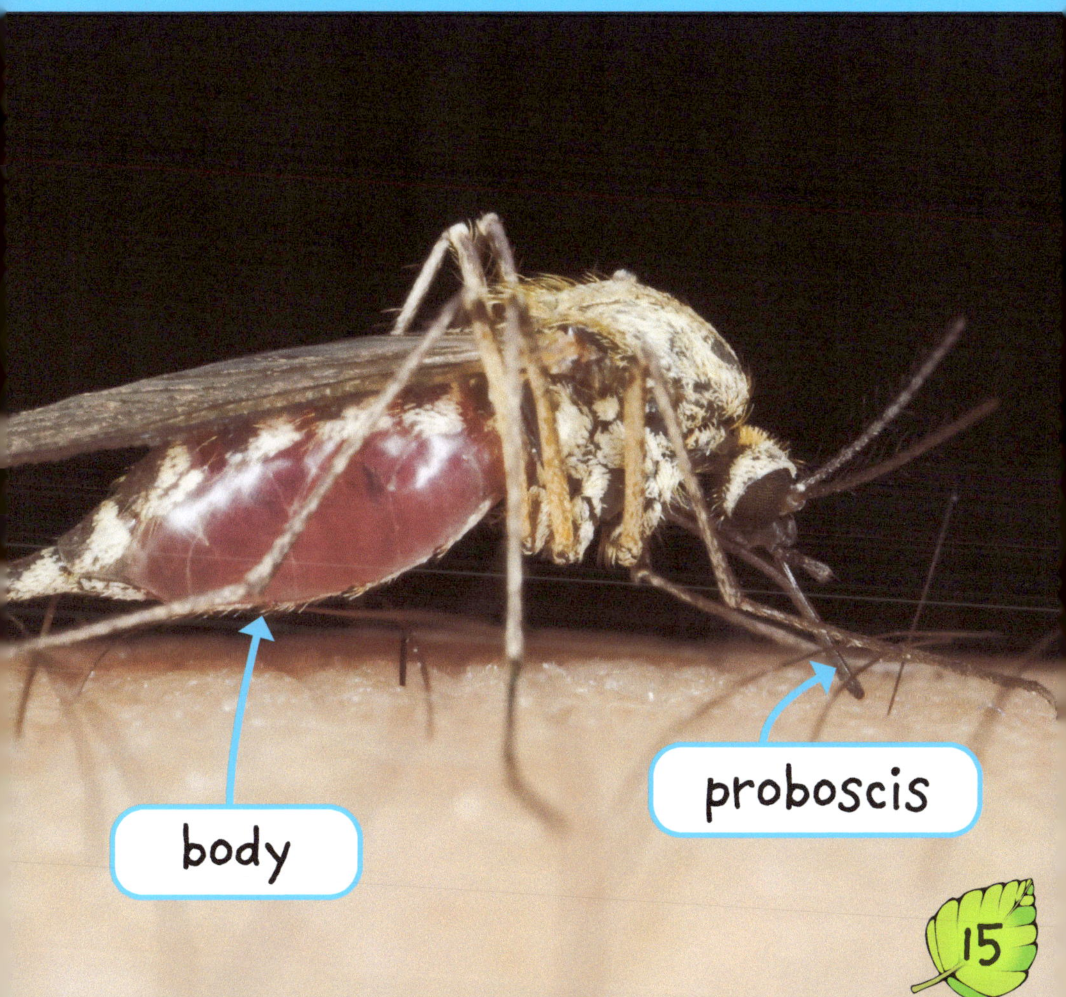

15

Moth

Pond Skater

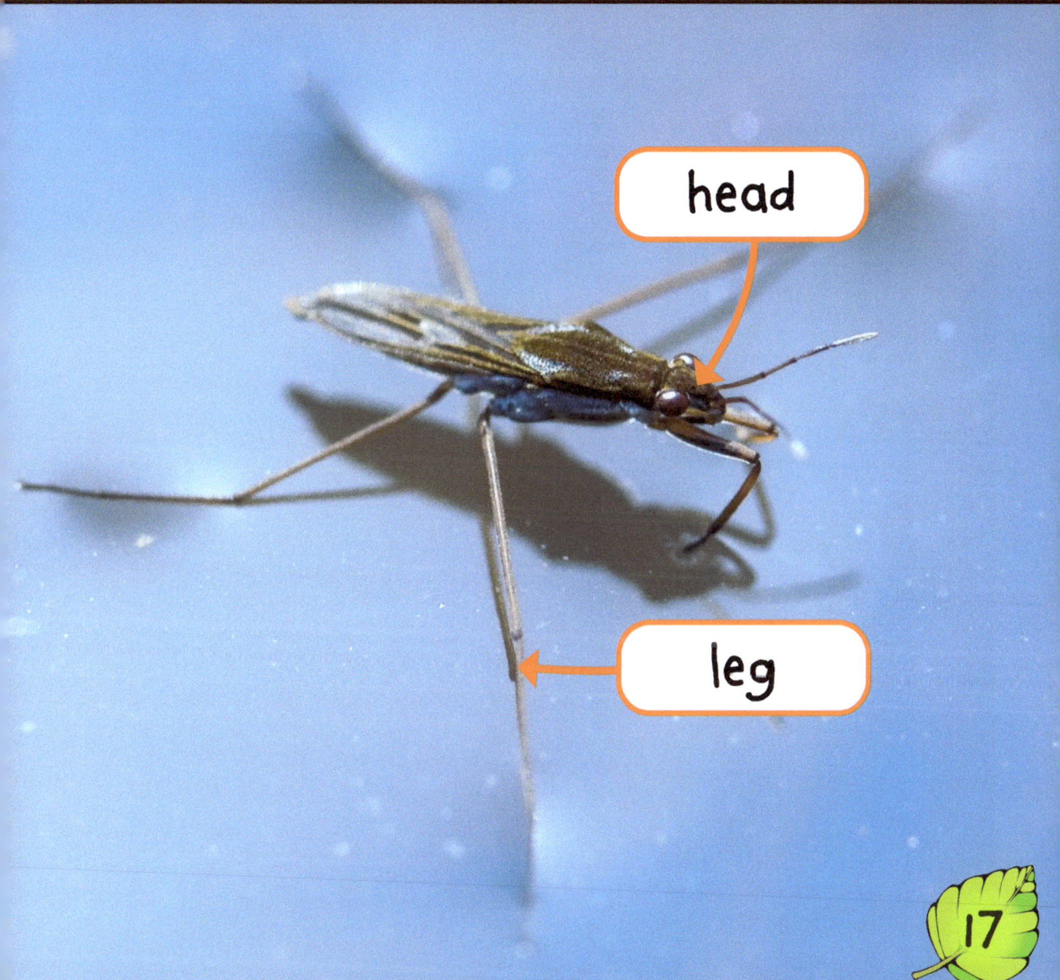

Praying Mantis

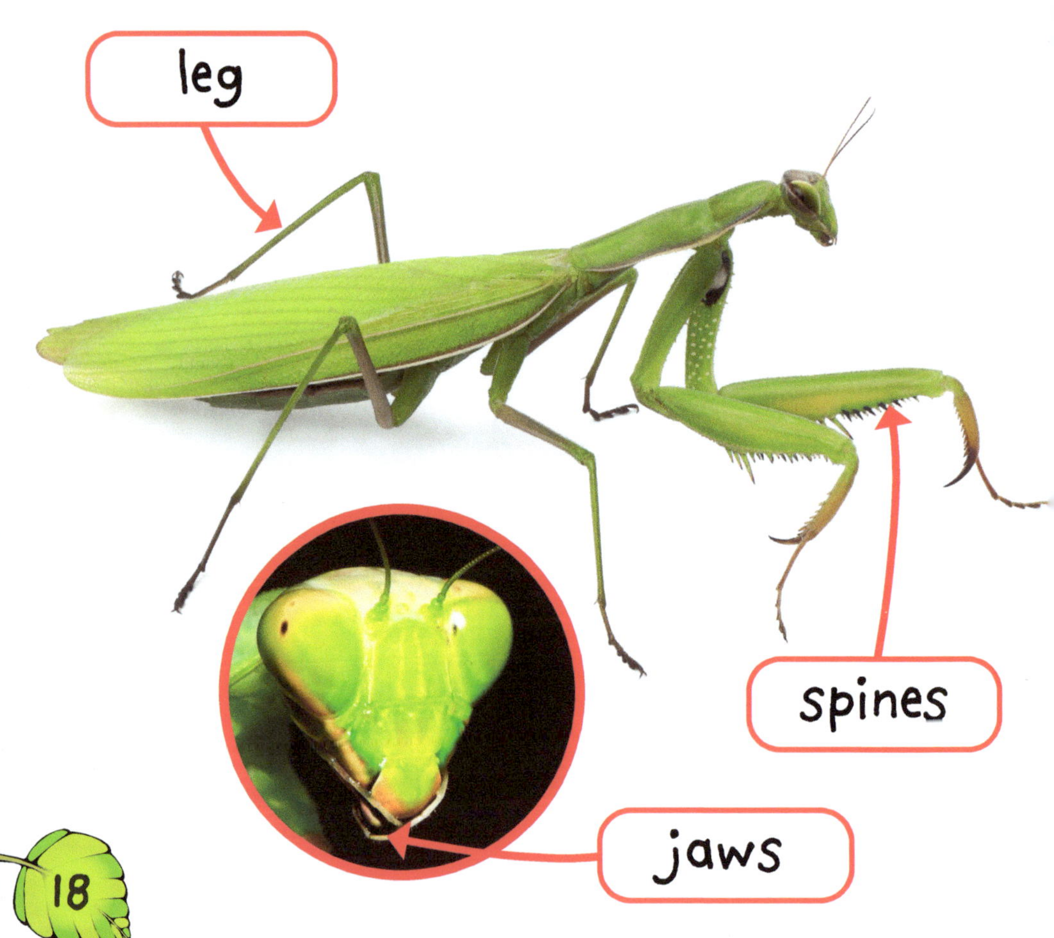

Silverfish

Stinkbug